Utterly Gorgeous CHRISTMAS

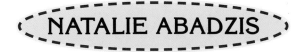

NATALIE ABADZIS

Scholastic Children's Books,
Euston House, 24 Eversholt Street,
London NW1 1DB, UK

A division of Scholastic Ltd
London ~ New York ~ Toronto ~ Sydney ~ Auckland
Mexico City ~ New Delhi ~ Hong Kong

Published in the UK by Scholastic Ltd, 2011

Text and artwork © Scholastic Ltd, 2011

Text by Natalie Abadzis
Illustrations by Natalie Abadzis
Art Editor: Katie Knutton
Photography by Simon Anning
Edited by Sally Morgan

ISBN 978 1407 120935

Printed and bound in Singapore

2 4 6 8 10 9 7 5 3 1

Utterly Gorgeous Contents

Things you will need

Here's all you need to make a cool collection of Utterly Gorgeous Christmas creations!

gold and silver card

white paper

coloured card and paper

napkins

curtain rings

tissue paper

craft glue

white card

postcard

sticky numbers

craft foam

pompoms

pinking shears

scissors

hole punch

envelopes

plant pot

newspaper

gold cord

felt or fleecy fabric

flower petals

tracing paper

glitter

wire ribbon

foil container

cocktail stick

potpourri

sticky tape

glue stick

ruler

rickrack

felt-tip pens

pencil

double-sided tape

glitter glue

black pens

hessian

paintbrushes

tags

canvas tote bag

embroidery thread

wrapping paper

cotton wool

needle and thread

gems

acrylic paint

sponge

plastic folder

sweets

sticky stars

nail scissors

doily

beads

fabric scraps

saftey pin

ribbon

baubles

sequins or sparkly shapes

chocolate coins

lolly sticks

buttons

Fabulous foil embossing

Give your handmade cards a touch of bling with fabulous foil embossing.

1 Stick Christmassy wrapping paper to a piece of card measuring 12 cm x 10 cm, and fold it in half.

2 Cut a piece of foil from an old food container. Place it on your work surface with a piece of scrap fabric underneath it.

3 Draw your design onto your foil using a pencil. Press your pencil into the foil fairly hard, to indent it with your design.

4 Cut out your foil design and attach it to your card with double-sided tape.

Choose Christmassy shapes such as stars, angels' wings or robins.

Beautiful baubles

Glam up boring or battered baubles with glitter, glue and gorgeous gift wrap.

1 Apply glue to the top half of your bauble using a paintbrush. Sprinkle glitter onto the gluey area until it's all covered. Do this over a piece of newspaper to catch any excess.

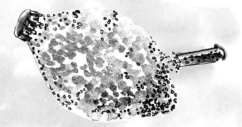

2 When your bauble is dry, apply a thin layer of glue to its bottom half. Sprinkle glitter in a contrasting shade onto the glue until it's all covered. Leave it to dry.

You will need

3 Thread some pretty ribbon through the top of your bauble and tie it in a loop. Hang your beautiful bauble on your tree. Gorgeous!

Cut cute shapes from gift wrap and glue them to your baubles for a decoupage design.

Printed napkins

Jazz up some dull paper napkins to give your table a fabulously festive feel.

1 Place your doily on the corner of a folded napkin.

2 Dip your paintbrush into the gold paint and wipe off any excess. Dab paint onto the napkin through the doily.

3 Carefully pull the doily away from the napkin and leave it to dry. Print a napkin for each guest. Bon apetit!

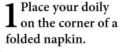

Napkin rings

You will need

Dine in style with these utterly gorgeous Christmas napkin rings!

1 Remove the little screw from the top of the curtain ring. Cut a long, thin strip of double-sided tape and wind it around the curtain ring.

2 Carefully, wind some Christmassy ribbon around each ring, so that it covers up all of the tape.

3 Tie a bow in another piece of ribbon and glue it to the ring. Make a napkin ring for everyone at the table.

Fanned Christmas doves

Spread peace this Christmas with these perfectly pretty paper doves.

1 Draw a dove shape onto a piece of white card and cut it out. Draw on an eye and some details with a thin black pen.

2 Make a slit in the middle of the dove's back with scissors. Measure and cut a 15 cm square of paper. Fold the paper over and back on itself several times to make a fan.

You will need

3 Carefully push the folded, fanned paper through the slit in the bird's body. Open the fan out, and glue the edges of the fan together, to make wings.

4 Fold a piece of ribbon in half and attach the ends to the back of the dove's wings using sticky tape. Decorate your dove with glitter to add some winter sparkle.

Try using brightly coloured card and paper, too.

Christmas love hearts

Don't you just love Christmas? Get into the spirit by making these fantastic, felt decorations.

1 Cut a large heart shape out of a piece of felt. Draw around the heart onto the felt and cut out another heart, the same size as the first.

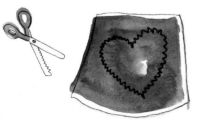

2 Cut a smaller heart from another colour of felt, using pinking shears. Glue it to the middle of one of the big hearts.

Try making love hearts in lots of different colours to make a whole set of beautiful decorations.

You will need

Make your hearts
even more lovely
with Christmassy
shapes and sequins.

3 Cut an even smaller heart shape from a third colour of felt. Glue it to the middle of the medium-sized heart. Glue the two big hearts together, leaving a space at the top.

4 Stuff the heart with cotton wool. Push the ends of a loop of ribbon into the gap at the top. Fix the ribbon in place and seal up the heart using glue.

Pantomime shoes

It's show time! For a Christmas tree with real star quality, decorate it with these fabulous footwear decorations, fit for a pantomime dame.

1 Trace and cut out the shoe template from page 62. Draw around the template onto a piece of craft foam twice, and cut out.

2 To make buckles, cut two squares from a piece of foam in a contrasting colour. Fold each square in half and snip a smaller square out of the middle.

You will need

3 Use a cocktail stick to dab some glue on the back of the gems and arrange them around the buckle.

4 Glue the buckles onto the shoes. Attach a loop of ribbon to the back of each shoe with sticky tape and hang them on your tree. Bravo!

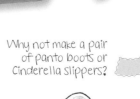

Why not make a pair of panto boots or Cinderella slippers?

Christmas stocking bunting

Use last year's leftover wrapping paper to make this gorgeous decoration for your mantelpiece.

1 Trace and cut out the stocking template from page 62. Draw around the main stocking template onto wrapping paper lots of times, and cut out the stocking shapes.

2 Draw around the toe, heel and stocking-topper templates onto more wrapping paper and cut them out. Stick these onto your stockings using a glue stick.

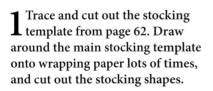

You will need

Use papers in contrasting colours to make a bold statement.

3 Arrange the stockings evenly along a length of ribbon or rickrack.

4 Glue your stockings in position and then leave them to dry. Hang your bunting from your mantelpiece, or drape it from the branches of your tree.

Christmas treat pots

Nothing feels more Christmassy than putting your presents under the tree. Why not make lots of trees and fill their pots with treats?

1 Paint the flowerpot with acrylic paint and leave it to dry.

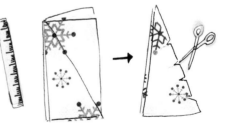

2 Fold a piece of Christmassy card in half and use a ruler to draw a line from one corner to the opposite folded edge. Cut along the line and then snip out lots of little triangles.

You will need

3 Unfold your tree and attach it to the back of your pot using double-sided tape. Decorate the tree with sequins and your pot with a bow.

To make your tree look extra special, choose sweets with pretty wrappers to fill your pot.

4 Glue a star to the top, and fill your pot with sweet treats. Yum!

Advent calendar

Can't wait until Christmas?
Count down the days with this
beautiful advent calendar.

1 Take a piece of hessian measuring
approximately 45 cm x 55 cm and
sew a 30 cm piece of ribbon to the top
with a needle and thread.

2 Using pinking shears, cut out 25 rectangles
measuring 8 cm x 7 cm from Christmassy-
coloured felt. Arrange these on your hessian,
then glue down the side and bottom edges,
leaving the top edge unglued to form a pocket.

3 Cut 25 seasonal shapes, small enough to
fit on the pockets, out of felt. Glue the
shapes onto the pockets. Add some gems
for decoration.

4 Use sticky numbers to number the
pockets 1–24. Now for the fun bit
– pop little treats into the pockets!

Add an extra treat to the last pocket for Christmas day!

Pretty paper wreath

These paper wreaths look so pretty, you'll want to make lots and hang them on every door.

You will need

1 Cut out the middle of the doily. Trace and cut out the small and large leaf shapes on page 62. Draw around your templates onto wrapping paper and cut them out.

2 Stick double-sided tape around the inner edge of the doily. Place one large leaf on the edge, then another next to it, until you have applied leaves all the way around.

3 Attach a layer of smaller leaves on top of the larger ones in the same way. Glue sparkly gems onto your wreath.

For a fuller looking wreath, add lots more layers of leaves!

4 Attach a loop of ribbon to the back of the wreath using sticky tape.

Nutcracker cards

Use pretty petals to make these scrumptious Sugarplum Fairy cards.

1 Place three petals onto your card. Use the petals as a guide to draw the head, arms and legs of your fairies with a thin black pen and felt tips.

2 When you're happy with your design, glue your petal tutus in position.

3 Add some Christmas fairy magic by adding spots of gold pen and sprigs of holly raining down from the fairies' hands.

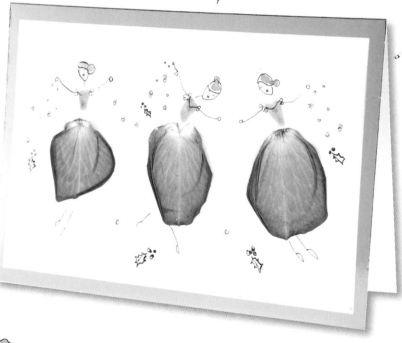

You will need

4 Stick the white card to a piece of folded gold or silver card and then take a bow!

Handy tip!
Try using other types of petals for the tutus and different numbers of fairies on your cards!

Christmas shopper

Got a friend who just loves to shop? Help her hit the high street in style with this sensational shooting-star tote bag.

1 Cut out a few felt stars and arrange them on your bag, but don't stick them down just yet.

2 Cut different lengths of golden rickrack to make the tails of your shooting stars.

Gorgeous gift alert!

3 When you're happy with your design, stick the stars and the rickrack to the bag with glue. Leave to dry.

4 To give the stars a bit of extra sparkle, glue on some beads and sequins. Magical!

Handy tip!
To make your design last until next Chritmas, fix it in place with fabric glue.

Gorgeous gift wrap

You will need

Jazz up plain wrapping with patterned snowflakes to give your gifts a more personalized look.

1 Cut lots of squares from patterned or glittery wrapping paper.

2 Fold each square into four and then round off the corner using scissors.

3 Cut different shapes into the edges of the folded paper. Unfold to reveal a beautiful snowflake. Make lots of snowflakes and glue them to a piece of plain wrapping paper.

4 Use your glammed-up paper to wrap your gift. Gorgeous!

Why not use more
snowflakes to make
some matching gift tags?

Lovely lanterns

Decorate your Christmas table with these pretty paper lanterns.

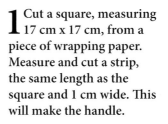

1 Cut a square, measuring 17 cm x 17 cm, from a piece of wrapping paper. Measure and cut a strip, the same length as the square and 1 cm wide. This will make the handle.

2 Fold the square in half lengthways, and then draw a line 2 cm away from one of the open edges.

Experiment with magic
lanterns in lots of
different sizes on your
Christmas table!

3 Make a cut from the folded edge up
to the 2 cm line. Repeat all the way
down the fold. Unfold the paper and
turn it through 90°. Roll up your
lantern and use double-sided tape to
stick the edges together.

4 Attach the handle inside the
top of the lantern using
sticky tape. Add some sparkle
with some sticky stars!

Gorgeous gift bags

The best things come in small packages, but they can be tough to wrap. Solve this problem with a gorgeous gift bag.

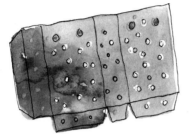

1 Trace and cut out the template on page 62. Draw around it onto some wrapping paper and cut out. Use a hole punch to make four holes across the top for the handles.

2 Fold your bag along the lines shown on the template. Use glue or double-sided tape to hold your bag together.

You will need

Perfect for your most precious presents.

3 Thread a 15 cm piece of ribbon through the holes in one side of your bag. Tie a knot in the ends, behind each hole. Repeat this for the other side.

4 Decorate your bag with sparkly shapes, or sequins. Pop some tissue paper inside, and it's ready for your gift!

Cute cushions

Sweet-smelling and super-cute, these pretty pillows make perfect presents.

1 Measure and cut a 12 cm x 24 cm piece of fleecy fabric and fold in half, lengthways.

2 Using a needle and thread, sew the open edges together leaving a gap so you can turn the cushion right-side out and stuff it.

3 Turn the cushion right-side out, and stuff with scented potpourri and cotton wool. Sew or glue the open edges of the cushion together.

4 Cut a stalk and leaf shape out of contrasting fabrics and glue them to your cushion. Cut an apple shape out of hessian and glue this on top. Stick on some buttons, and there you have it!

Glue on any shapes you like. Try an orange or a pear shape, with fruity potpourri.

Robin Redbreast place cards

Make everyone feel welcome at Christmas dinner with these adorable robin place cards.

Rockin' robins!

1 Fold a piece of Christmassy card in half. Cut out a smaller rectangle of green card, and glue it to your card at an angle.

Handy tip!

To make your place cards look extra special, write your guests' names into the green boxes in gold or silver pen.

2 Trace and cut out the robin templates on page 63. Draw around the main robin template onto a piece of brown paper. Cut the robin out.

3 Draw around the redbreast template onto a piece of red craft foam or paper. Cut it out and stick it onto your robin's tummy.

4 Stick your robin onto your card. Draw your robin a beak, an eye and some legs with a black pen.

Stationery gift set

Brighten up a friend's thank-you letters with a sensational stationery gift set.

You will need

1 To make a star design, cut out lots of stars from assorted wrapping paper and glue them to the top of the writing paper and envelope.

2 Outline the stars with a thin black pen.

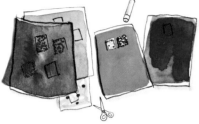

3 To make a present design, measure and cut out lots of squares measuring 2 cm x 2 cm from assorted wrapping paper. Glue two squares, in different colours, to the top of each sheet of writing paper.

4 Glue one square to the flap of each envelope. Outline all the squares with a thin black pen, and add some bows so they look like beautifully wrapped gifts.

Handy tip!

Why not decorate some postcards, too?

Chocolate coin purses

No need to empty your purse to make these presents. Yum!

1 Cut a simple purse shape out of a piece of folded felt. This will give you two shapes. Make sure it's big enough to fill with chocolate coins.

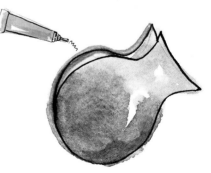

2 Glue the edges of your purse together. Leave the top open so you can get your coins in and out.

You will need

Glue on any shapes you like and make purses in all different colours.

3 Cut a little Christmassy shape from felt and glue it to the front of your purse. Stick on some stars or sequins.

4 Lastly, fill your purse with chocolate coins and tie it up with pretty ribbon.

43

Snowman bookmark

You will need

You might not get a white Christmas, but you can still make snowmen!

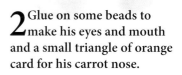

2 Glue on some beads to make his eyes and mouth and a small triangle of orange card for his carrot nose.

1 Glue two white pompoms 1 cm from the top of your lolly stick.

Bling up your snowman with bold buttons made from gems or sequins.

4 Cut a hat shape from card and glue it so that it covers the top of your stick. Tie a bow around the middle of your bookmark to make it look extra fancy.

3 Make a scarf from a scrap of ribbon and glue it around the snowman's neck to keep him warm.

Handy tip!
Paint your lolly sticks before you start for a more professional look.

Gorgeous garlands

Designer labels you can afford!
Get tag-tastic with these
gorgeous garlands.

1 Cut out some Christmassy shapes from coloured gift wrap. These could be snowflakes, fruit, gifts or trees.

2 Glue the shapes onto your tags using a glue stick.

You will need

3 With a thin black pen, draw an outline around the shapes. Make your outline slightly off centre for a retro feel.

4 Thread some lovely ribbon through the top of each tag and tie them to a long piece of string or ribbon.

Christmas candy canes

These are the kind of sweet treats you can't eat, so you can use them again next year!

1 Trace and cut out the candy cane template on page 63. Draw around the template onto a piece of coloured craft foam, and cut it out.

2 Trace and and cut out the white stripes from white foam. Attach them to the cane with double-sided tape.

You will need

Add glitter for some bling!

3 Wrap a piece of ribbon around the cane. Tie into a bow and snip the edges diagonally so they do not fray.

4 Use sticky tape to attach a loop of ribbon behind the cane to hang it on your tree!

Reindeer silhouettes

Hang these reindeer silhouettes at your window to remind Santa to stop by.

1 Measure and cut a 15 cm x 20 cm piece of card. Trace and cut out the template on page 63.

2 Place the template on the centre of your card and draw around it. Use nail scissors to cut out the reindeer shape.

You will need

Santa stop here!

3 Attach some wrapping paper, patterned-side down behind the reindeer, using sticky tape.

4 Attach a loop of ribbon to the back of the card with double-sided tape. Decorate your silhouette by gluing on a little bow and some festive sequins.

Russian dolls

Dress up your pressies with these picture perfect dolls!

You will need

1 Trace the doll templates on page 63. Draw around the templates onto a plastic folder with a permanent pen. Cut the doll and face shapes out with a border around them. These will be your stencils.

3 Place the face shape onto the doll shape and dab on either yellow or red paint. Leave to dry. Draw a face, bow and detail with a black pen.

2 Use sticky tape to attach the doll stencil to white card. Use an old sponge to dab on yellow or red paint. Leave to dry.

4 Cut out your tag with a border around it, and enough room at the top to punch a hole. Punch a hole in the top and push through a piece of ribbon.

Beautiful babushkas!

Handy tip!
Why not make some in different sizes?

53

Get your skates on!

Don't skate around the issue … make these ice-cool tree decorations!

You will need

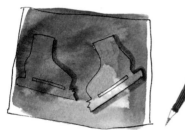

1 Trace and cut out the template on page 63. Draw around the template, onto a piece of foam twice.

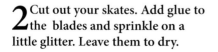

2 Cut out your skates. Add glue to the blades and sprinkle on a little glitter. Leave them to dry.

3 Use a cocktail stick to glue on some gems for the lace holes. Add a sticky star to each boot.

4 Lastly, attach a loop of gold cord to the back of each skate using sticky tape.

Beautiful birdcage

These sensational songbirds will look utterly gorgeous perching in the branches of your Christmas tree. So 'tweet'!

You will need

1 Trace and cut out the template on page 64. Draw around the template onto a piece of silver paper and cut out your cage.

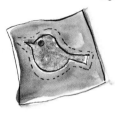

2 Cut a small bird from wrapping paper and glue it onto a piece of felt. Cut it out again, leaving a border. Glue on a sequin eye.

3 Tuck the bird into the cage, then glue the bird and cage onto some gold card. Cut it out, leaving a border and tab at the top.

4 Punch a hole in the tab and thread through some ribbon.

Snowflake brooch

Bling on the bad weather! Brighten up even your most boring, winter outfit with this sensational brooch!

You will need

1 Trace and cut out the template on page 64. Draw around the template onto sparkly paper and cut it out. Stick on some gems for a bit of bling.

2 Glue the snowflake onto a piece of felt. Cut it out, leaving a border. Repeat this with felt in another colour.

3 To attach a safety pin to the back, glue a piece of felt through the pin, covering the side that doesn't open.

Woolly hats and mittens

Wrap up your Christmas tree with these winter warmers!

1 Trace and cut out the hat and mitten templates on page 64. Draw and cut around the templates onto folded blue felt so you have four mittens and two hats.

You will need

2 Decorate one of the hats by adding sticky stars and pieces of ribbon. Stick a pompom on top. Glue a loop of gold cord behind the hat, and glue the second hat to the back of the one you've decorated.

3 Decorate two of the mittens with a sticky star and glue on a piece of ribbon.

4 Glue the mittens to each end of a piece of ribbon. Glue the two extra mittens to the back of the decorated ones.

Handy tip!
Why not try making different types of hat?

59

Doily angel

Make a beautiful angel for the top of your Christmas tree – or stick her on to a Christmas card!

1 Fold a doily in half, then in half again. Fold over the top edge and wrap it around a lollystick and glue into place.

2 Add glitter to the edge of the doily for a magical sparkle. Draw a face on the top of the lollystick.

3 Wrap and glue some embroidery thread around the top of the lollystick for some hair. Glue on a piece of ribbon for the top of the dress.

4 Make angel wings by cutting a piece of 10 cm wire craft ribbon. Bend in half and glue to the back of the lollystick.

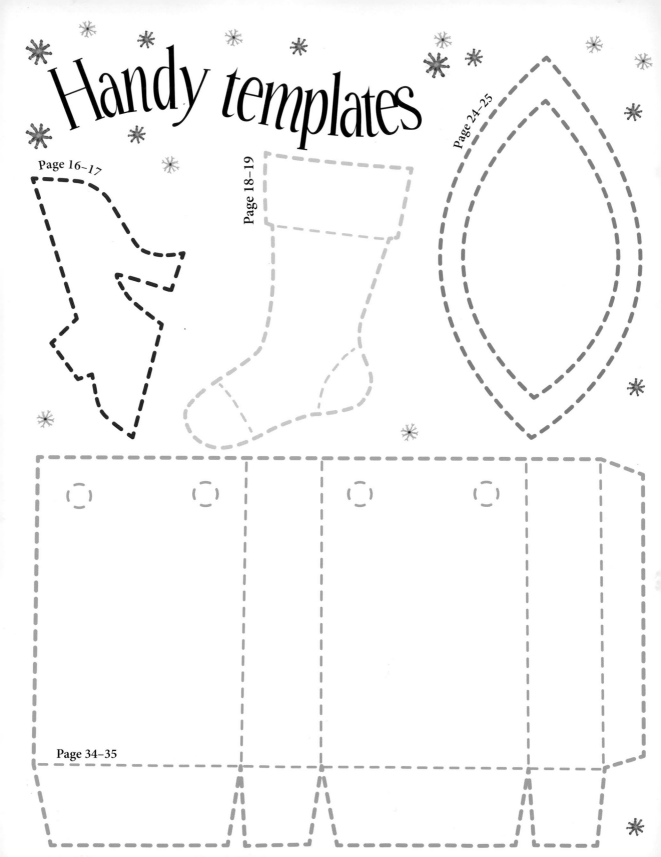

Handy templates

Page 16–17

Page 18–19

Page 24–25

Page 34–35

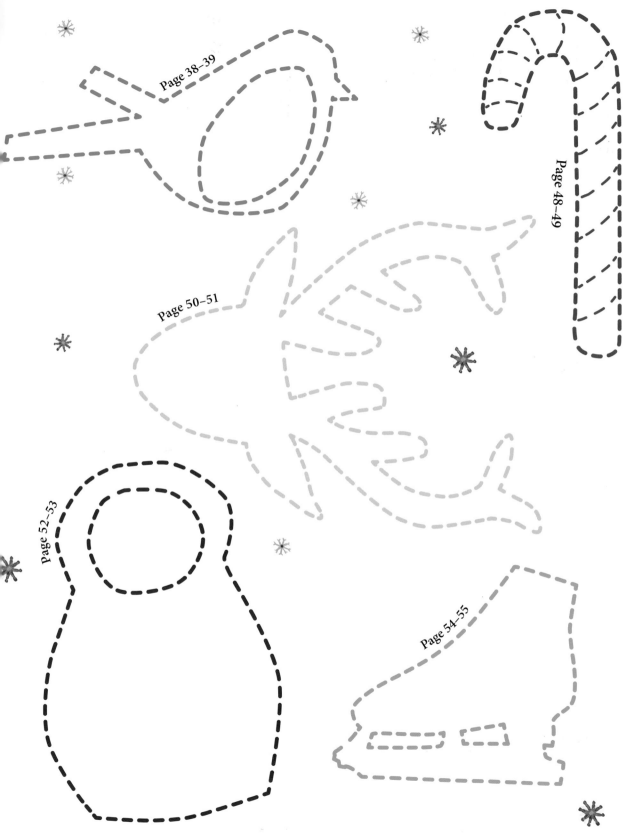

Page 38–39

Page 48–49

Page 50–51

Page 52–53

Page 54–55

Page 57

Page 56

Page 58-59

Dove

Christmas shapes

Heart

Star

Bell